Mark's books are filled with important, humorous and insightful anecdotes derived from his years as a gymnastics coach and parent. His books are a wonderful way to learn what is really important about gymnastics and life.

Michael & Susan Jacobson
U.S. Gymnastics Training Centers Summer Camps

Going For It! "2"

A Second Gym Bag Companion For Living Our Dreams

*This book is dedicated to
Timmy and Brianna.
Two dreams come true.*

D1317869

Other Great Going For It! Books By Mark Gibson

Going For It! "1"

The original book by Mark that has taught thousands of gymnasts how to train like champions.

Price $16.95

Going For It! "2"

The sequel to Mark's first book. More inspiring wisdom for every gymnast with a dream.

Price $16.95

The Going For It! Workout/Meet Journal

Comes in a sturdy 7" by 9" 3 ring binder. 100 workout pages. 15 meet pages. Fun to use. A real champion's tool.

Price **$17.95** (Specify girls' or boys' when
Refills **$9.95** ordering or girls' will be sent)

Shipping and Sales Tax: *U.S. Orders add $3 first item, 50¢ for each additional.*
PA Add 6% Sales Tax
CANADA - Call for pricing.

Mail orders to Wind Dancer Publications PO Box 263 Perkasie PA 18944

To order direct from the publisher call: **215 257 4584**
(Gym Club Discounts Available)

More than
150 clubs
a year bring,
Mark Gibson's
inspiring
live
program
to their
gym

A seasoned traveler at just 18 months, Timmy Gibson had already crossed the country twice and traveled through more than 30 states. Now, when Mark goes on tour his entourage includes Timmy's little sister Brianna as well as mom Donna.

Call for details (215) 257-4584

Going For It!

A Second Gym Bag Companion For Living Our Dreams

Copyright © 1998 by Mark Gibson/Wind Dancer Publications

Published by Wind Dancer Publications

United States Publication: June 1998

ISBN 0-9644172-8-6

Wind Dancer Publications
P.O. Box 263
Perkasie PA 18944 USA

215 257-4584

A special thanks to...

Steve Elliott for his enthusiastic support of my first book. By sharing GFI 1 with so many fellow coaches it quickly became a huge "word of mouth" success.

Doc. Massimo, Peter Vidmar, Mary Lee Tracy, and Mike and Susan Jacobson for their feedback on the manuscript of GFI! 2

Joe Ferry and Cindy Trauger for helping me weed out the glitches and typos.

All the gymnasts and coaches who responded to the GFI questionnaire. You all provided me with a wealth of inspiring insights. I'm sorry I couldn't include all your quotes. Cassie Abel, Stephanie Aloi, Cheryl Auger, Vanessa Baland, Ashley Bard, Allison Betof, Christie Black, Mandy Bonas, Ashlee Bradley, Rebecca Burdick, Kayleigh Burns, Amanda Busher, Caitlin Cain, Bethany Cavedon, Gina Candora, Erin Cardin, Anna Caucci, Jill Chandler, Rachel Clunie, Emily Conner, Becky Clement, Kelly Detweiler, Kristi Dobra, Kelsey Dow, Katharine Eckert, Karen Erickson, Diana Fields, Whitney Ferguson, Erin Filisko, Jamie Freman, Ashley Gable, Cassie Gainay, Katie Gofus, Michelle Goldkamp, Leigh-Anne Gross, Allison Horne, Skylar Inman, Evan Jones, Roxanne Jones, Ashley Julien, Krystal Kasperitis, Lauren Kellett, Shannon Kellett, David Kenny, Julie Lamar, Holly Landry, Jessica Lepionka, Nicole LeFebure, Christina Lupacchino, Amanda Martin, Kimberly Martin, Amy Mason, Heather Miner, Lisa Mortensen, Tara O'Neill, Ian O'Roourke, Jane Marie Page, Megan Petrie, Kelliane Piel, Cristine Perry, Krista Polmounter, Justine Rehak, Miranda Rothrock, Stefanie Rousselle, Ashlea Sattarwhite, Tina Seward, Julie Shaffer, Nikki Shaffer, Kelly Smith, Lauren Smith, Caitlin Stephan, Patty Stotzhiem, Kelly Straka, Jessica Strocky, Sarah Tomlinson, Amanda Tompkins, Kate Uorne, Brittanie Valipour.

Didn't see your name in the list above? I received several questionnaires back without the name and gym club section filled out. Opps!

Thanks to the coaching staff at Bucks II, Fallington PA; YWCA of Northern R.I., Woonsocket RI; Gymnastics and More, North Myrtle Beach SC; Greenville Gymnastics Training Center, Greenville SC, and Orlando Gymnastics and Cheerleading, Orlando FL.

And mostly to Donna. Thanks for sharing my passion for the uncommon life.

CONTENTS

CONTENTS (continued)

Life
is either
a
daring adventure
or nothing

- Helen Keller

Forward

Gymnastics is a very tough sport both mentally and physically, but it often comes down to who is toughest mentally. We included a lot of sport psychology in our training on our road to the Olympics. We wanted to be sure our minds were ready for the competition of our lives -- the Olympic trials. Mark's first book, Going For It! has been used in our gym [Cincinnati Gymnastics] by coaches, athletes and parents. It makes sports psychology easy and fun. We both read Going For It! in one day and continued to refer to it leading up to the Olympic trials. We found it easy to read, but more importantly it taught us valuable lessons about how to train and compete at our best.

GFI! 2 is as good as, if not better than, GFI! 1.

We both want to say a special thank you to Mark for making a difference in our careers.

AMANDA BORDEN and JAYCIE PHELPS
Atlanta Olympics Gold Medal Team

CHAPTER 1

DREAMS

Zap! Weeeee! Wosh! Clang!
Walla Walla Walla! Crash!

Making Your Own Future

On Three; Ready, Set, Go!

Be A Little Better Than Your Best

Don't Confuse Wishes For Wants

Dream Your Own Dreams

Keep A Learning Journal Of Your Journey

Save Your "Warm Fuzzies"

Create A Dream Shrine

Become Your Heroes

Mentors

Support Someone Else's Dreams

Everyone
Moves Towards
The Future
They Create Today

What Kind
Of A Future
Am I
Creating For
Myself?

ZAP! WEEEEE! WOSH! CLANG! WALLA WALLA WALLA! CRASH!

"I don't dwell on the bad. I think of all the great new things to come."
Leigh-Anne Gross - Level 9

You are startled out of a deep sleep one night by a strange sound. You open your eyes and there sits Doc. Brown. You know, the guy from the Back to the Future movies. You climb aboard his time machine and fly off into the future.

You land at an NCAA championship meet some time in the future. Looking around the gym floor you notice one gymnast who looks oddly familiar. Yep! It's a 20-year-old you. And wow, do you look good. Is that really you warming up a full twisting Tsukahara? Is that really you nailing a double back on floor? And is that really you catching two different releases in the same bar routine? Yes! Yes! And yes! It really is you.

Things get even weirder. You actually get to speak to yourself. "How did I get so good?" you ask your 20-year-old self. "You worked for it," your 20- year-old self replies. "You mean all I have to do is come in the gym every day, work hard, stay focused, and keep improving and I will end up being this good?" you wonder. "Yep. That's about it," a taller you replies. " I won't kid you, it's gonna be a struggle. You'll consider quitting a couple of times, and there will be some real down moments. But in the end it will all be worth it."

"Wow," you think.

I have a clear picture in my head of the kind of life I want.

Winners
Make Their
          Future Happen
Whiners
Let Their
          Future Happen

MAKING YOUR OWN FUTURE

"My dream is to work with dolphins and use my gymnastics in an act with them."
Ashlee Satterwhite - Level 6

When you go to the gym the next day following your trip through time and back, you find yourself training a little differently. You are taking more turns. During those turns you tend to concentrate more on form and technique than you normally do. Between turns you don't want to "hang out" at the chalk bin, chatting about nothing. Instead you notice you are wandering off by yourself to think about your next turn up.

When your coach gives you a correction you listen intently. A fellow gymnast is working on the same skill and without really thinking about it you start asking questions about the skill.

Why are you so willing to work this hard today?

Maybe it's because you are 100% clear on where you are heading, you know what you need to do to get there, and you don't feel like wasting your time on anything that keeps you from your dream.

Welcome to the world of a winner.

I move a little closer to my dreams at every workout.

The Three Most Important Questions
All Winners Ask Themselves:

What...
> Do I Want?

How...
> Am I Going To Get It?

When...
> Am I Going To Do Something
> About It?

ON THREE; READY, SET, GO!
"People told me I wouldn't be able to make the [level 9] team.
I tried my all and I made it."
Mandy Bonas - Level 9

Winners, it seems, have figured out the three essential steps for chasing dreams:

Winners know what they want to be

Winners know what they have to do

Winners get on with what needs to be done

To put it another way:

Winners have...

A Dream

A Plan

A Commitment

Sure I know what I want, and yes I've figured out how to get it,
but most importantely, I do something about it.

Aim
For 10% Higher
Than What's
Realistic
For You

BE A LITTLE BETTER THAN YOUR BEST

I wanted to show my coaches that I was ready to move up to level 7.
I set 4 goals for myself, and reached them all."
Katharine Eckert - Level 7

With sufficient desire and motivation we could all be Olympic team members, right? Well, no! We all are born with different levels of natural ability. By the time most gymnasts reach 12 years of age they have a pretty good idea of where they stand competitively.

Just making it to level ten (girls) or level one (boys) would be a tremendous achievement for some. For many, a college gymnastics scholarship is a goal that would require an enormous amount of effort. For others, aiming for a spot on the national team would be a stretch. And yes, some could push themselves all the way to the Olympics.

Dreaming dreams is a delicate art. If we set outrageously high, unrealistic goals we may quit in frustration, convincing ourselves we are worthless in the process. Set them too low and we may never come close to reaching our full potential.

The best bet? If it truly inspires you to train hard, then go ahead and dream about Olympics. But when it comes to everyday training, set achievable goals that will inspire you to stretch a little beyond what you think you are capable. Think maybe you'll be doing a twist on floor by the end of the season? Then train like a gymnast who wants a double twist. See a tuck Tzukahara vault in your future? Then train like a gymnast aiming to learn a layout Tzukahara. Pretty sure you're going to make it to states? Then train like you're going to qualify for regionals.

I move in the direction of my dreams by focusing on the next 45 minutes.

Wishes
Are The Things We
  Think We Want
But...
     Are Not Willing
To Do Anything About

DON'T CONFUSE WISHES FOR WANTS

"There are lots of things I wish I could be, but right now I want to be a
great gymnast so that's what I focus my time and energy on."
Amanda Cooper - Level 10

Jenny says she wants to qualify for regionals this year.

That's what she says, but what she does about it doesn't seem to match.

Jenny is scheduled to work out 5 times a week but lately she's been lucky if she gets in 4 workouts. You see, it's track and field season at school and Jenny is a great sprinter, so she's been putting in a lot of extra hours after school to get her 100 meters time down. She's also looking forward to doing a little cheerleading.

Jenny's words may say she wants to go to regionals, but the fact is she really just wishes she could go to regionals. Her actions are telling the truth. Jenny really wants to be a good all-around athlete.

Is there anything wrong with being a good all-around athlete? Absolutely not. If that is what truly gives Jenny the most satisfaction, then that may be the right choice for her.

However, Jenny must face the reality that she can't "have it all." She must focus her energy on what she truly wants and accept that wishes only come true in fairy tales.

I wish I could be a five feet, ten inch tall supermodel,
but I want to be a four feet, ten inch tall supergymnast.

Dreams
Without Action
Are As Powerful As
An F-15 Jet Fighter
...Without Fuel

FUEL YOUR DREAMS

*"I keep by biggest dreams written down on a
piece of card that I carry with me everywhere I go."*
Monica Smith - Level 8

Dreams are like a bicycle.

Without you constantly pushing the pedals around, even the fanciest high tech bicycle in the world would just sit there, going nowhere. Same thing goes for dreams. The dreams you have today will continue to inspire you a year from now only if you constantly develop and build them.

Champions have learned to keep themselves motivated day in and day out, through tough workouts and learning slumps that seem to last for months. How?

By keeping their dreams alive and right in front of them. They write them down and keep them in their gym bags or posted around their bedroom mirrors where they can read them everyay.

They know that if they ever allow their problems or distractions to become bigger than their dreams they are probably going to start thinking about quitting. Champions carry around powerful dreams to constantly remind them why they are working so hard, and why they are sacrificing so much. They know that without a dream to make it all worthwhile, gymnastics can be a frustrating way to spend a big chunk of their lives.

My dreams are like a campfire. I will never let mine go out.

When You
Are Committed To Learning
Teachers
Suddenly Appear
From
Everywhere

KEEP A LEARNING JOURNAL OF YOUR JOURNEY

"I have a 3 ring binder. I call it my book of lessons. I write down every important lesson I learn so that I don't forget it and have to relearn it 6 months later."
John Haliday - Level 1

Every day commit yourself to writing down at least five things that you learned.

This will change the way you train forever. *I guarantee!!!*

Imagine if at every workout you knew you had to come up with no less than five things you learned that day. You would listen better. You would ask more questions. You would take more turns and make more corrections.

What did you learn from watching others, from pushing yourself harder, from listening to your coach, from falling off beam/pommel horse 27 times?

In other words, your workouts would not be about "trying." They would be about learning. At meets, you'll want to know what you can learn from the kid on "that other team" who throws hissy fits and cries through half the meet? At workout, what did that pre-school kid teach you about having fun? What did that 15-year-old class gymnast teach you about determination when she made her first kip ever today?

Choose a journal that you really like, one with a cool cover and fancy paper. This is going to be one of the most important tools in your gym bag, so don't just scribble your lessons on the back of an old school notebook.

I don't like learning the same lesson over and over. I learn it once, write it down and remember it.

Keep Your Dreams Alive

SAVE YOUR "WARM FUZZIES"

"When I read my fan mail and see how many
people support me it keeps my dreams alive."
Whitney Ferguson - Elite

In my office file cabinet I have I have one file marked "warm fuzzies." This file is stuffed with hundreds of letters I have received from gymnasts. There are letters from all over the U.S. and Canada, from England, and even some from Australia. I call them my "warm fuzzies'' because reading them gives me that "warm fuzzy" feeling.

Every letter is from a gymnast who read my first book and wanted to let me know how it has affected their lives.

Whenever I read these letters I am reminded about why I took the bold move to quit my full-time coaching job to become a writer and speaker. They give me the courage to stick with my dreams despite all the setbacks and challenges.

A "warm fuzzy'' can be any reminder of a past accomplishment. Medals, ribbons, newspaper clippings, meet score sheets, meet programs, note and cards from parents or friends... anything that inspires you and helps to keep you track of your dreams.

I know I'll keep my "warm fuzzies" forever. Start collecting yours today.

With all the things that go wrong in training and competition it's easy
to forget all the good stuff that happens. I don't let that happen.

Set Aside
A Small Space
Dedicated
To
Your Wildest Dreams

CREATE A DREAM SHRINE

"I get two copies of USA Gymnastics magazine.
One to keep and one to cut the pictures out."
Jennifer Landi - Level 8

Dedicate one small corner of your bedroom to your dreams.

All you need is a flat wall and a small shelf.

Cover the wall with a collage of anything that inspires you. Things such as photos of your favorite gymnasts, posters of Olympians or national team members, inspiring quotes from famous people (not just athletes) and "stuff" collected from your gymnastics road trips.

Put at least three framed pictures on the shelf. One of you doing something you are proud of (winning a medal, or even just an action shot of you on the apparatus.) Another of you with your team, and one of you with your family. The shelf will also contain inspiring books that you have read, and your collection of "warm fuzzies."

Surround the whole thing with any medals and ribbons you have won.

This little corner of your room will become a constant reminder of your dreams and a place you can go for inspiration. Remember to change things around and add new bits and pieces as often as you can. After a while old stuff becomes, well, old.

My dreams are my responsibility.

Do Not
Idolize Your Heroes

Learn
From Them

BECOME YOUR HEROES

*"When I saw that poster of the mens' Olympic team posing
with their shirts off I stopped whining about conditioning."*
Mark Gilbert - Level 3

There are two ways of looking at our heroes.

1. We can see them as god-like creatures who exist on a higher plane than normal human beings.

2. Or we can see them as regular people who are fortunate to have been born with the right combination of talent, opportunity, and determination.

When we raise our heroes to the level of untouchable supermen and superwomen we also degrade ourselves. Thus, our heroes are people we admire because they have superhuman qualities we mere mortals could never hope to obtain.

A better idea is to see our heroes as determined, hard working, mistake-making ordinary people. While it's true that we may not have been born with their extraordinary talent, we still can develop all those other qualities we admire so much. Things like courage, perseverance, and compassion.

By seeing our heroes as ordinary people with extraordinary determination we can be inspired to be more like them. By seeing them as superhuman demigods we assume their is nothing we can learn from them.

My heroes are not above me, they are just ahead of me. I can catch up.

Just
As Plants Grow Towards
The Sun
People
Grow Towards
Those They Admire

MENTORS
"This would be a lot harder without my sister to look up to."
Jane Wallace - Level 9

One of the benefits of being a team-oriented gymnast is recognizing that other people can teach us a lot, but only if we let them. Our coaches are always going to be there helping us to do our best, but sometimes we need a different kind of advice. We need to speak to someone who really seems to understand what we are going through.

This is where mentors come into the picture. A mentor is a person we can turn to for advice. A mentor is a trusted friend who listens well and who has already been through many of the obstacles and hardships we are facing. A mentor is always someone we admire, look up to and respect; a person we want to be just like.

Often, a young gymnast sees something in an older teammate that reminds them of themselves. Perhaps a beginner level competitor admires the dedication of a 16-year-old optional gymnast on their team. A friendship is struck, and now that younger gymnast has someone they can turn to for advice. The biggest plus to this relationship is that it works two ways. Both the young beginner and the older, more experienced competitor benefit.

Can you figure out how?

I have the desire, you have the knowlege; let's inspire each other.

Support
The Dreams Of Others
and
they will
support yours

SUPPORT SOMEONE ELSE'S DREAMS
*"You can't fake concern for your teammates.
It has to be genuine or they'll see right through you."*
Andrew Carter - Level 2

One of the most important steps you can take to achieving your dreams is to dedicate yourself to helping other people achieve their dreams.

You probably are thinking it takes all the time and energy you have right now just to pursue your own dreams. When are you going to find the time to help other people?

The fact is, no one can achieve their dreams alone.

> *A single snow flake falling on a city street will have no effect whatsoever. However, when that same snowflake gets together with a few billion of his buddies together they can close down the entire city.*

This is what happens when team members share similar dreams, and all are moving toward the same goals. When you support your teammates' dreams, they will support yours and together you will have a combined strength of commitment far beyond what any one of you could obtain alone.

Somehow my dreams don't seem so crazy when I'm
surrounded by people who think the same way I do.

WHAT THIS CHAPTER MEANS TO ME

1. When I think about the kind of gymnast I want to be in 10 years I have:

　　A... *a clear, detailed picture in my mind, and specific goals written down.* ☐

　　B... *an idea. I mean I want to be good but I'm not sure how good.*............. ☐

2. What I get from gymnastics will be the result of what I work for, not what I wish for:

　　A... *I agree with this statement 100%.*... ☐

　　B... *well yes, but if you can cut corners here and there, why not?*............... ☐

3. I enjoy watching gymnastics on TV because:

　　A... *those performances inspire me to work harder at my own dreams.*....... ☐

　　B... *it's fun to watch stuff I'll never be able to do.*............................. ☐

4. My dreams:

　　A... *are my responsibility. I do everything I can to keep them alive.*............. ☐

　　B... *depend on who ever happens to be motivating me, coach/parents/friends.* ☐

5. I see my teammates' dreams as:

　　A...*a reason to share my inspiration with others.*................................. ☐

　　B... *a threat to my own dreams.*... ☐

What does this tell me about the power of my dreams?

THE LAST WORD

Everything starts with a dream.

Imagine you live in Key West, Florida and you want to take a cross country drive. The initial step is to come up the idea in the first place -- that's the dream. Next, you have to get specific. Where do you want to finish? Los Angeles, San Francisco, Seattle, Anchorage? Without a clear destination you could wind up anywhere. Let's say you decide to aim for San Francisco.

Next, you have to plan the route. Without a plan you may just head straight up the East Coast to Boston. So you get a map, you speak to people who have already done the trip, and you start to plot out all the cities and towns you need to pass through. Finally the planning is done. It's time to hit the road. So you start driving, not to San Francisco, but to Miami. From Miami you aim for Tallahassee, and then New Orleans. You always keep San Francisco in the back of your mind but each day you are aiming for your short range goal -- the next big city.

After a week or so you make it to San Francisco. You succeeded because you started with a dream, turned it into a plan, followed the plan by achieving small successes along the way, and this encouraged you to keep pushing forward towards your eventual dream -- San Francisco.

CHAPTER 2

TRAINING

Train Like A Champion And Your Dreams
Will Take Care Of Themselves

Permanent Potential

Gambling On Your Own Greatness

Everyone's An Expert At Something

Raising Your Standards

Listening

Asking Questions

Taking Notice

Getting The Job Done

Socialize Less

Take More Turns

Get Comfortable With Being Uncomfortable

Stop And Think

A
Meet
Is Not Won
At The Meet!
It Is Won
At The
Workout

TRAIN LIKE A CHAMPION AND YOUR DREAMS
WILL TAKE CARE OF THEMSELVES

"I always keep in mind the reason I am at the gym."
Amanda Busher - Level 8

Lazy Loni has this gymnastics thing all figured out.

"I come in to work out as often as is convenient. Then, at those workouts, I do just enough work to keep the coach from losing his cool. It's a very skillful art. I have to know just how much slacking off and goofing around the coach will tolerate before he starts yelling.

At the meets, and only at the meets, I try a little bit harder. I keep my arms straight on the press to handstand. I straighten my legs on my handspring vault. And I even attempt to stick a few landings. I could do all these things at workout, but imagine how tiring that would get. Now and then I win a few ribbons and medals. There is a down side. Every season it seems my teammates move up a level while I get left back. I'm not thrilled about that, but at least I don't have to work as hard, right? Hey! You can't have it all."

Imagine how good Loni could be if she tried as hard at workouts as she does at meets.

I pay the price for my dreams with hard work and commitment.

It
Really Doesn't Matter
How Good You Could,
Should Or Would Be...

It Only Matters
How Good You
Are

PERMANENT POTENTIAL

"I know I won't move up [to the next level] unless I train hard."
Ashley Julien - Level 4

Do you know someone who suffers from permanent potential?

It's that false sense of security some gymnasts have that allows them to never actually perform up to their potential. "After all," they will tell you, "I could be good if I wanted to."

Why wouldn't anyone want to perform up to their full potential? Good question. Maybe they think it's too hard. Perhaps they don't have powerful dreams to push them. Or maybe they are scared that if they really went all out and trained like a winner they may realize one of their greatest fears - that they really aren't as talented as they think. Then the secret would be out. Everybody would know Mandy is mediocre, Alex is average and Olivia is ordinary. What a nightmare! Better to have people believe in their potential than to discover the possibility they are just another struggling gymnast.

So instead of developing their talent they develop their excuses. Mandy is always injured, Alex is too stiff in the shoulders for rings, and Olivia can't tumble because she's too tall.

They are all going to be great some day. Just not today, thank you very much.

The belief that I could be good is a fine place to start, but a bad place to get stuck.

Never
Let Today's Dreams
Become
Tomorrow's Regrets

GAMBLING ON YOUR OWN GREATNESS

"I enjoy learning new skills because once I learn them I feel so good about myself."
Amy Mason - Level 5

To really tap our greatest potential means facing one of life's biggest fears: that maybe our dreams are bigger than our abilities. Hardly seems fair, does it? In order to find out just how good you could be at anything you have to push yourself to the edges of your ability. And that means if you give your best and still fall short of your dreams you will spend the rest of your life feeling like a big old failure. All that hard work would be for nothing, right?

Wrong!

Surprise, surprise! The biggest regret most people have in their lives is not that they failed, but that they failed to try.

This is what being in sports is all about. It's not just about winning but also striving to win. It's not just about getting the gold but also going for the gold. And it's not just about being the best, it is also about being our best.

Yes, it's a gamble. Some athletes avoid the risk of failure and all the yucky feelings that come with it. They've discovered that by training and competing way inside their potential they can enjoy the recognition of being a player without everyone putting too much pressure on them to perform. Clever?

If this is such a clever system, why are these people so unhappy most of the time?

I'd rather fail giving it 100% than to never try at all.

We All
Become Experts
At What We Practice Most

Good

Or

Bad

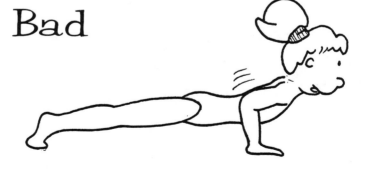

EVERYONE'S AN EXPERT AT SOMETHING

"It's frustrating; learning new skills.
You just want to do them perfect the first time."
Ian O'Rourke

What kind of expert are you?

Some gymnasts are experts at keeping their legs straight. Others are masters of basic swing. Some are proficient at pointing their toes.

Some gymnasts are experts at bending their legs. Others are masters of the arched handstand. Some are proficient at the bent arm vaulting.

How did they all become experts? Everybody becomes an expert the same way.

By practicing.

If you come into the gym and spend five years practicing bent leg cast to handstands, you will become an expert at bent leg cast to handstands. Guaranteed!

If you come into the gym and spend five years practicing straight leg cast to handstands, you will become an expert at straight leg cast to handstands. Guaranteed!

It's a real simple system. You don't need to be an Einstein to figure it out.

Killing time is killing opportunity. I make the most of every minute of every workout.

Starting Today...
Expect
A
Little More
From Yourself

RAISING YOUR STANDARDS

"If I give 100% on tough days I can get through anything."
Ashlee Bradlee - Elite

Cory's coach really bugs her sometimes. Like when she comes off the apparatus, her coach always makes some comment about her legs being bent or her head being in the wrong position. And when she's right in the middle of an important conversation with her friends, her coach will actually suggest that she walk away from the chalk bin and go do some annoying drill. It's really starting to work on her nerves.

The problem between Cory and her coach is clear. She and her coach have different standards for how much work should get done during a workout.

Winners have a simple rule.

Never have lower performance standards than your coach.

If the coach expects 5 routines. Winners willingly do 5 routines. No fussing... no whining...no complaining...they just do them. Not because they are blindly obedient little servants too scared to say no. They do them because they share their coach's commitment to excellence.

They have the same high expectations as their coach, so they do what needs to be done.

No one has to make me work hard.

Listening
is
the first step of
learning

LISTENING

"There are days when I don't feel like listening to anyone.
Those tend to be the days I get very little done."
Rachel Donner - Level 10

We all listen to our coaches, don't we? I'm not so sure. How many times have you heard a coach's voice getting louder and louder as he attempts to correct a gymnast on vault? The reason? She's already walked half way back up the runway, right in the middle of what the coach was saying. Talk about rude.

How does a winner listen?

- A winner looks at the person speaking to them.

- A winner acknowledges the speaker (a nod, smile or a "Yep!" will do.)

In other words, listening requires the listener to actually do something.

Ignoring our coaches is a non-verbal way of saying "I'm really not that interested in what you have to say." This is a surefire way to encourage the coach to start ignoring us.

The last thing I want to do is turn off my main source of feedback. I always listen to my coach.

The 5 Most Important Tools For Learning Are:

HOW... (do you do that)?
WHY... (do you do that)?
WHAT... (can I do to learn that)?
WHEN... (do I need to do that)?
WHERE... (do I need to do that)?

ASKING QUESTIONS

"One of the coolest things I every did was meet Shannon Miller.
She was so nice and answered all my questions."
Stacy Potter - Level 8

A great way to encourage anyone to share information with us is to ask questions.

Winners want to understand every aspect of their training, so they ask a lot of questions. They ask fellow gymnasts how they perform a particular skill. They ask judges (away from the meet, of course!) how they want a pose to look. And they ask their coaches all manner of questions about technique and form.

Do they ask questions after every turn and every routine? No! That would drive even the most patient coach bananas. They only ask questions when they sincerely need extra information.

They don't ask questions in an attempt to impress the questioner. ("Gee, if I ask lots of questions people will be so impressed with my desire to improve that they won't notice I spend more time talking than working." Oh, yes they will.)

Only ask questions when you sincerely want to hear the answer.

I never assume I know it all.

Teachers
Are All Around Us
We
Just Have To
Open Our Eyes
And See Them

TAKING NOTICE

"I assume everyone I meet can teach me something."
Gregg Anderson - Australian gymnast

What is your left pinkie finger doing right now?

Notice how you suddenly became aware of your left pinkie finger when I brought it to your attention. Until then, your left pinkie finger was just one of the thousands of things your brain was selectively ignoring.

This is how your brain works. As amazing as that super-computer in your noggin is, it could never handle every piece of information that your five senses bombard it with. So it filters out all the stuff it thinks is not important to you.

When you stroll into the gym without a clear set of goals in your head, your brain responds by helping you focus on things like chatting with your friends or daydreaming.

However, when you arrive at the gym with your head full of all the skills, drills and thrills you are going to experience, your brain makes that a priority. Now, all of a sudden, you are noticing other gymnasts performing the same skill. You listen in on other gymnasts' coaching tips. You pay closer attention to your own body and what it is doing. Your brain understands that performing well and learning is important to you, so it makes you aware of all those things in the gym that can help you.

At school I'm tuned into studying. At the gym I'm 100% gymnastics.

Actions
Really
Do
Speak Louder
Than
Words

GETTING THE JOB DONE

"I was scared about doing a back walkover.
After I just got up there and did it, it was easy."
Jill Chandler - Level 5

So we are listening to our coaches and asking occasional questions. Surely our coaches must be impressed with our apparent desire to succeed?

Not yet they won't.

There is one more step. We also have to do something with the information. Point that toe. Turn our heads differently. Alter our body shape slightly. Whatever! Nothing makes coaches want to tear out large clumps of their own hair more than a gymnast who looks right at them, seems to listen, nods, then does the complete opposite.

There are little retirement communities in Arizona where they send coaches who went crazy trying to get their gymnasts to keep their legs straight on back walkovers.

You probably didn't know that, did you?

No one expects perfection after one correction, but at least an attempt at a change keeps the coach wanting to help us more.

I always do a little bit more than what's comfortable for me,

They Don't Call Them Socialouts

SOCIALIZE LESS

"I talk to the "chatty" ones, but I don't let them get to me.
I still have my work to do."
Cheryl Auger - Level 6

If you are like most gymnasts, you probably have a lot more in common with your gym friends than you do your school friends.

By the time you get to the gym you can't wait to share the day's news. Somehow, the gravitational pull of the chalk bin draws you in and before you know it you are chatting about the day and forgetting to take turns.

But remember, they don't call these sessions workouts for nothing. The general idea is that "working" is the first priority. Chatting comes second.

Probably a good 80% of the socializing we do could be eliminated altogether. It's just idle chit-chat anyway. The other 20% can be taken care of before and after workout, or during apparatus changes.

When chatting during workout, try to keep the conversation based on gymnastics.

Sure I want to catch up on the news, but work is priority #1.

Take An Extra Turn Every 15 Minutes

TAKE MORE TURNS

*"Tough days are the ones that make me a stronger
gymnast, both physically and mentally."*
Skylar Inman - Level 10

Do the math with me here. It gets confusing, so read slowly. Let's say on average you get about one turn up on the apparatus every 90 seconds or so. Each turn lasts about 10 seconds. So that's about 10 seconds of work every minute and a half... or 100 seconds of work every 15 minutes... or 1,000 seconds of work every 150 minutes (in other words about 16.5 minutes of work every two and a half hours.) The other two hours, thirteen minutes and 30 seconds is standing around time.

Now let's say right here -- you do have to rest between turns. But...what some smart gymnasts have already figured out is you don't have to train five times harder than the next gymnast to get the advantage. If you could just take one extra 10-second turn during every 15 minutes of a two-and-a-half hour workout, that would add up to an extra 100 seconds per workout (not much, eh?). For a gymnast working out 4 times a week, 50 weeks a year that would add up to an extra 20,000 seconds of work a year (that's 333 extra minutes). Remember, it used to take two and a half hours to do 16.5 minutes of work. So 333 extra minutes is like getting an extra 20 workouts a year. That's more than a month's worth of work!!!

How many times have you gone to a meet thinking, "I wish I had one more month to get ready for this?'

Well, now you do.

More turns = more opportunities to learn. Who can't understand that?

Hardships
Are Temporary
But
Pride
Lasts Forever

GET COMFORTABLE WITH BEING UNCOMFORTABLE

*"I motivate myself by thinking about my dreams
and knowing that my competitors are working hard."*
Kelly Smith - Level 10

No one likes to feel uncomfortable. However, the only way to get better at anything is to push ourselves to the edges of our abilities. If we come into the gym every day and never do anything new, we never learn or improve. So doing things that are a little scary, hard, and frustrating is an unavoidable part of learning.

My wife Donna came up with a great technique for dealing with discomfort when we were touring Europe on bicycles one summer. On cold, wet miserable days spent pumping up the side of some Spanish mountain on very heavy touring bikes, Donna would remind me that by 10:00 PM none of this hardship would matter. By then we would be in our tents, snuggled into sleeping bags, dry and warm. And we would be stronger, more determined and better cyclists.

Our motto for that trip became:

Hills don't last forever but memories do.

Same goes for the gym. Conditioning doesn't last forever. Working flexibility doesn't last forever. Learning slumps don't last forever. Bad meets don't last forever. Ripped hands don't last forever. The list goes on. If we push ourselves through the hardships of training we come out stronger and more determined.

The strength of character I develop from pushing through discomfort will last forever.

Practice
Every Skill Mentally
Before
Attempting It
Physically

STOP AND THINK

*" I would never climb up on beam without a clear
picture in my head of exactly what I wanted to do."*
Allison Newly - Level 10

This is a biggie!

I am going to share with you a tip that will improve the way you train faster than anything else.

Here it is:

**Spend at least as much time thinking about your next
turn as you do performing the actual turn.**

That's it. It's that simple.

Before every turn take 10, 20, or 30 seconds to walk off quietly by yourself and visualize in your head the skill you are about to attempt. Think about the technique -- what shape will your body need to be in? Think about the form -- toe point, legs straight, body tight.

Don't ever climb onto the apparatus without a clear and vivid picture in your head of exactly what you need to do.

If I'm not thinking... I'm sinking!

WHAT THIS CHAPTER MEANS TO ME

1. On skills that I can already perform well I always keep perfect form:

    A... *true*... ☐

    B... *false*.. ☐

2. In general, I expect more from myself than my parents and coaches do:

    A... *true*... ☐

    B... *false*.. ☐

3. I encourage my coaches to help me by listening and making corrections:

    A... *true*... ☐

    B... *false*.. ☐

4. My coach never has to call me away from the chalk bin for a turn. I am always ready:

    A... *true*... ☐

    B... *false*.. ☐

5. I always take at least 10 seconds to visualize my next turn before attempting it:

    A... *true*... ☐

    B... *false*.. ☐

What does this tell me about how I train on a daily basis?

THE LAST WORD

Imagine yourself sitting on a bicycle. Your coach starts pushing you until you are going quite fast. You are probably thinking that you could not go any faster. Then you notice the pedals.

You start pedaling like crazy. Soon you are going so fast that your coach can barely keep up. Now you don't need your coach to push you. Instead, he bikes along side offering tips about head position and pedaling style. You listen to his advice, make the changes, and speed up even more. As you fly down the road you begin to notice other gymnasts. They are sitting on their bicycles with their feet dangling down. Their poor coaches are pushing as hard as they can but you can see they are losing patience. You shout, "Use the pedals. Move yourself." But they don't seem to understand. Eventually, those coaches stop pushing and the other bikes all coast to a stop. The gymnasts get off and quit in frustration. "Why didn't everybody push me harder?" they each complain.

Meanwhile, you are zipping along with the wind in your hair, and having a great time.

This is how coachable gymnasts train. They let their coach put their energy into improving them, not pushing them. They are working hard, they are in control, and they are having fun.

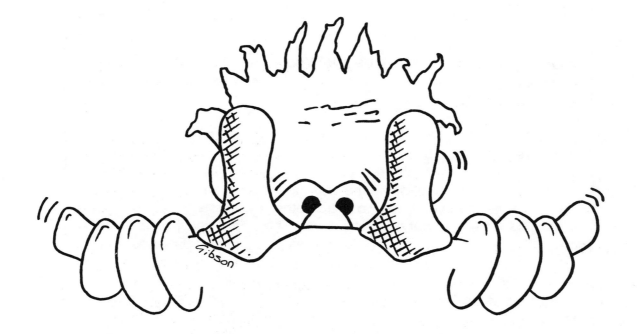

CHAPTER 3

CHALLENGES

Careful What You Wish For

Learn Gymnastics In 10,000,000 Easy Challenges

A Healthy Diet Of Challenge

Overcoming Challenges Makes Us Stronger

Obstacles Or Stepping Stones To Greatness?

Get Scared More Often

Start Making More Mistakes And Make Them Sooner

Disappointment

Injuries

The Challenge
Is What
Makes It Fun

Without
The Challenge
Why Bother?

CAREFUL WHAT YOU WISH FOR

" I used to wish gymnastics were easier so I could learn faster.
I now know that's pretty pointless."
Barry Forman - Level 1

Imagine you pick up an old Snapple bottle on the beach one day. You unscrew the cap and out whooshes a genie. "I may grant you one wish," he proclaims. Without a second thought you reply, "I want to be able to perform any gymnastics skill I can imagine." "Consider it so," says the genie, and promptly disappears into the clouds like a mini-tornado.

"Wow!" you think. "This is going to be so cool."

Your next workout is unbelievable. Double layout on floor? No problem. How about a triple twisting double layout? You got it. OK! next turn up, a quadruple layout with six twists and a rebound double front out. Stuck!

This sort of thing goes on for a month. At the end of the month you quit gymnastics. "What? Quit? Are you nuts?" your friends all ask. "I have to," you reply "gymnastics is boring.

There is nothing left to learn."

The reason I love gymnasts is, there is always something else to learn.

Gymnastics
Is Just One Problem
After Another
Or
One Exciting
Challenge
After Another...

Depending On Your
Attitude

LEARN GYMNASTICS IN 10,000,000 EASY CHALLENGES

"There is never an end to the challenge. It's like the Energizer Bunny,
it just keeps on going and going."
Mandy Bonas - Level 9

So you spend an entire summer trying to learn a full twist on floor. Six zillion into an open pit. Another forty two zillion onto a mat in the pit. Seventeen zillion with a spot on the floor ex'. Then, the day arrives. Your coach steps back and says "OK, now try one by yourself."

You nail it!

Everyone goes nuts. Your coach gives you a high five. Your friends are around you, and you feel great. Finally, you have a full twist. You can finally take it easy.

Less than a month later your coach casually mentions "Hey! wadda ya say you try an' learn a double." So you start all over again. Pit...mats in pit...floor with spot....

Problems, problems, problems, or challenges, challenges, challenges?

Depends on your attitude.

Problems are a burden, challenges are a staircase.

So
You Know
What You Want
But
Do You Know
Why
You Want It?

A HEALTHY DIET OF CHALLENGE
"Challenges are what make the sport fun and exciting."
Justine Rehak - Level 5

Many gymnasts think they know what they want. They want a kip, or a giant, or a full twist. But have they stopped long enough to think about why they want it?

"Because it'll make me feel good," is a popular answer. OK, so they don't really want the kip. What they really want is to feel good. The kip, giant or full twist is just a way to achieve that good feeling. In other words, it's overcoming the challenge that is the real reward.

Think about it this way. We keep ourselves alive physically by taking in food and water. Without food and water we wouldn't last very long, would we? Well kips, giants and full twists help to keep us alive emotionally.

While our bodies need daily doses of food and water our minds need daily doses of challenge to stay healthy. Without an exciting challenge to move toward our lives are quite dull.

Some gymnasts don't realize this, and they are emotionally starved most of the time. They complain about having to go to gymnastics, they whine about conditioning, and they are not a lot of fun to be around.

These poor, under-nourished people are starving for a challenge and they don't even know it.

I get hungry for challenge.

The Pride
Of Accomplishment
Will Be
In Direct Proportion
To
The Challenges
Overcome

OVERCOMING CHALLENGES MAKES US STRONGER

"Overcoming fears are the biggest challenge."
Heather Miner - Level 5

Did you ever stop to think how strength training makes you stronger? You pick up a heavy weight and your brain says, "Wow, put that sucker down before you hurt yourself." So you put the weight down. But then you pick it back up again, and put it down, and pick it up, and so on. Eventually, your brain reluctantly accepts the fact that you are going to keep picking up this stupid weight. So it tells your muscles to adapt their abilities to handle the new weight. And you become a tiny bit stronger. (I know it's a little more complex than that, but this is not Biology 101, for Pete's sake.)

This is pretty much the same way it works for anything. If you frequently push the outer limits of your ability, you get a little better. Of course, if you push too hard, you get into trouble. (Pick up too much weight -- you pull a muscle, throw a double tuck dismount off bars the day after learning giants -- you land on your noggin.)

The trick is to constantly look for challenges to stretch toward. Challenges that are a little bit beyond your current abilities.

It's the challenges I overcome that make me stronger.

Opportunities Come To Us Disguised As Challenges

OBSTACLES OR STEPPING STONES TO GREATNESS?

*"Trying your hardest is the greatest challenge.
Not trying 50%, but more like 150%."*
Holly Landry - Level 7

Winners not only expect to be challenged frequently along the road to their dreams, they actually seek out challenges. Winners know that the more challenges they can defeat, the stronger they become.

Winners live their lives on the edges of their abilities. As a result, winners are always putting themselves in situations that test them. So winners get scared often. Winners make a lot of mistakes. Winners mess up all the time. And winners learn from all these experiences, gain more confidence, then go right out and take on even more daring challenges.

Winners don't see the challenges of life as obstacles. They see them as stepping stones. They know that the only way they can possibly make it to their dreams is to become stronger, more confident and courageous. And that doesn't happen sitting at home, sucking down a Slurpee, and playing video games every night.

Winners know that every mistake is an opportunity to learn something. Every fear is a chance to develop courage. And every disappointment can fire them with even more determination.

Without challenges to keep me strong I would sink into mediocrity.

Every Fear
I
Overcome
Moves Me Closer
To My
Dreams

GET SCARED MORE OFTEN

"You can be the most talented gymnast,
but if you are afraid to try new skills you will never progress."
Amanda Busher - Level 8

Think about it for a moment. When do you get scared?

Doing skills that are easy? No, of course you don't. You only get scared trying new skills or doing something that is a challenge.

That means you get scared only when you are pushing yourself. And guess what? You get better only when you are pushing yourself. So it looks as though fear and improving go hand in hand. You can't have one without the other. Bummer, eh?

Winners understand this. They don't run away from their fears. They know if they do they are also running away from their dreams.

Winners actually get kind of excited about fear. They know they must be at the edge of their abilities and on the verge of learning something new. So they concentrate and do whatever it takes to keep moving forwards safely to their dreams.

I don't avoid fear I deal with it.

If You Can't Do It Right...
At Least
Make A New Mistake
Before The Old One
Becomes
A Habit

START MAKING MORE MISTAKES AND MAKE THEM SOONER

"My dad always says can't means won't."
Erin Filisko - Level 5

Do you love doing puzzles?

I do. My favorites are the three dimensional kind. Some are as simple as two metal nails twisted into a loop and linked together. Others are far more complicated, made of wood, rope, and metal. I now have a collection of them. I've done them so many times that I can zip them apart like a real pro. It wasn't always this way. Whenever I get a new puzzle it takes me minutes (sometimes hours) of clanging and banging those things around until I finally separate the two parts or remove the metal ring.

I've learned not to get frustrated by failure. I know that learning how to do these dumb little puzzles means having to make mistake after mistake after mistake. I have to try hundreds of ways that don't work until I can learn what does work and solve the puzzle.

Gymnastics is the same way. If we get too caught up in our mistakes we might not see them for what they are -- opportunities to discover what does not work. Winners expect to make lots of mistakes when they are learning something new. They take as many turns as possible so they can make all their mistakes in as little time as possible. Every time they make a mistake they ask themselves what they learned from that mistake. Then they get right back up and try again.

If I'm not making mistakes it usually means I'm not trying hard enough.

Occasional
Disappointment Makes
A
Winner
Even More
Determined

DISAPPOINTMENT
"Knowing what you did wrong means you know what to do to change it."
Allison Horne - Level 4

Want to make sure you are never disappointed ever again?

Simple!

Just lower your expectations. That's it. Once you give up on the idea of ever being a good gymnast you will never again go to a meet and get upset.

Hey, so you sat down on your vault. Big deal! So you fell off beam/pommel horse 27 times. No problem! So you over-rotated you first pass on floor, ran backwards off the mat, stepped into a chalk bin, tripped over the judges table, and landed in the judges lap. What a riot!

Does this sound like the attitude of a winner?

Frankly, I would have a problem with a gymnast who never cared about messing up or performing poorly. When we take pride in our performance it's only natural to feel somewhat bummed out about blowing a meet or failing at something.

If you feel disappointed all the time then it's possible you do have unrealistically high expectations for yourself. You may need to chill out a little. However, if you are only occasionally disappointed then congratulations, that's normal -- and healthy.

Disappointment reminds me that I care about what I'm doing.

Ignoring
Injuries
Makes About
As Much Sense
As Ignoring
A Fire Alarm

INJURIES

"The only time I wish gymnastics were easier is when my knees hurt."
Lisa Mortensen - Level 5

Does your body talk to you?

Sure it does. Maybe it doesn't use the English language but it talks all the same. When your body needs to rest it lets you know by speaking quietly. It makes you tired.

If you ignore your body it speaks a little louder by giving you small aches and pains.

Ignore this warning and your body raises its voice. It throws a slight injury at you -- a rip, or maybe a sore muscle.

Finally, unwilling to be ignored any longer your body gets rather demanding and stops asking you to rest. Instead it says "We're resting, darn it." This is how we end up with sprained ankles, torn ligaments and other even more serious injuries.

Of course, a small number of injuries are the result of just rotten bad luck. But most are foreseeable and avoidable if we would just listen to all the warnings our bodies give us.

The whole key to improving as fast as possible is to push the edges of our limits. Injuries are our bodies' way of reminding us that we have pushed ourselves way past our limits. So our bodies cleverly take control of us and pull us back into our limits again by forcing us to rest -- one way or another.

I always listen to my body.

WHAT THIS CHAPTER MEANS TO ME

1. I wish gymnastics would be less challenging:

    A... occasionally.. ☐

    B... frequently.. ☐

2. When I think about past challenges I have overcome I am:

    A... grateful I had the opportunity to grow stronger from those challenges ☐

    B... grateful that they are over... ☐

3. When I think about all the challenges that still lay ahead for me I get:

    A...excited... ☐

    B...depressed... ☐

4. I view my mistakes as:

    A...a chance to learn what doesn't work and make corrections............... ☐

    B...evidence that I am hopeless.. ☐

5. I look upon injuries as:

    A...a reminder to balance the needs of my body with the needs of my dreams. ☐

    B...as an excuse to quit my dreams altogether............................. ☐

What does this tell me about how I view the challenges of gymnastics?

THE LAST WORD

So the key to being a real winner in life does not depend on the result of your last meet. Being a real winner is a daily process. A winner is a winner 8,760 hours a year. (Yes, even when they are asleep. Winners know how important it is to get good rest.)

Winners have figured out what they want to achieve. They know what they want to be in 10 years and they know what they have to do today to get there. But winners are not so hung up on their goals that they can't be happy until they achieve them. In fact, quite the opposite is true. Winners have learned that once a goal has been reached there follows a letdown sort of feeling, and that they need a new goal to get them excited again.

In other words, it's not the goal itself that makes all the hard work so worthwhile, it's the striving for the goal that is the real benefit. Achieving the goal is just life's way of saying "OK, you're done, now start something else."

Now here is the odd thing. Focusing on the process of winning as much as the win itself is a surefire way to win more often.

CHAPTER 4

CONFIDENCE

Confidence Is More Important Than Talent

Real Confidence

Accumulating The Right Experience

The Going For It! Confidence Loop

Confidence Taker #1 - "I'm Not Good Enough"

Confidence Taker # 2 - Comparing Yourself To Others

Confidence Taker # 3 - Fear

Confidence Taker # 4 - Failure

Confidence Taker # 5 - Self-Doubt

Confidence
Is Not
The Certain Knowledge
That You Can Do It
But
The Belief
That You Will
Figure Out
How To Do It

CONFIDENCE IS MORE IMPORTANT THAN TALENT
"I believe I can make it happen if I work hard."
Anna Caucci - Level 4

Go to just about any gymnastics meet in the country. Check out who gets to go up on the award stand. In the younger age groups(7 to 11 year olds) the award stand will be full of naturally gifted and super-talented kids. Now stick around for about 5 years and check out the same meet.

Where did all those super talents go?

Some are at diving meets. Some are dancers. Some are cheerleaders. And a handful are still competitive gymnasts. The fact is, gymnastics is a very tough sport to be in. It requires a level of dedication and commitment that very few adults could handle in their jobs. So a lot of very talented gymnasts quit. Why? Well, some due to injuries, but many because they lacked the determination to keep going.

Determination is strengthened by confidence. Confidence is developed through achieving many small and meaningful accomplishments at every workout and at every meet.

Very often it's not the most talented gymnasts who end up as champions. More often, it is the ones who had the confidence to believe in themselves and the determination to overcome all the obstacles they lay between them and their dreams.

Confidence lets me take the next step, then the next, then the next...

You
Don't Lack Confidence
Because The Skill Is Too Hard

The Skill Is Too Hard
Because You
Lack Confidence

REAL CONFIDENCE
"A lack of confidence is just your body reminding you that you haven't done the work."
Ron Grainger - Level 2

"OK Becky and Brenda," says the coach, "today's the day you guys do your first double backs on floor without a spot."

Becky takes a big gulp. She is so scared. She has spent the entire summer landing on her knees in the "resi-pit." She can get over to her feet on the floor but only if her coach gives her a real heavy spot. But she really wants to do the double back, so she tells her friends to start "psyching" her up. She gets herself "pumped up" by pacing around and by jumping up and down in the corner of the floor ex'. After she's balked about six times, her coach gets mad at her and starts yelling. This is good. She needed someone to yell at her to get her through this. Eventually she runs like crazy and "chucks" her first double.

Brenda does things a little differently. She spent most of the summer landing on her feet in the "resi-pit." It took more effort, but she figured the extra effort would pay off when it came time to do the skill by herself on the floor ex'. She is feeling a little nervous, but not what she would call scared. She knows she is ready. Instead of getting "psyched," "pumped." or yelled at, Brenda simply takes about three minutes to walk off by herself. With her eyes closed she runs perfect double backs through her mind. Just like the dozens she has already done into the pit. As she stands in the corner of the floor she imagines she is facing the pit. She tells herself that she can do it, and she does it -- perfectly -- the first time. Three months later, Brenda competes her double back. Becky is not at the meet. She injured her ankle at Thursday's practice when she landed a little short on her double back.

My confidence doesn't come from winning a big meet. It comes
from hundreds of small corrections leading up to the big meet.

Self-Confidence
Is A
Reasonable
Expectation
Of Future Events
Based On
Past Experience

ACCUMULATING THE RIGHT EXPERIENCE
"Nothing compares to feeling prepared when it
comes time to check your confidence."
Allison Betof - Level 9

Confidence is that sincere feeling of faith in our ability we get by having completed the entire process of learning a skill. In other words, hours of conditioning, five million drills, two million times being spotted, etc. It is then that a picture begins to form in our minds, a picture of success, and we are confident we can do it.

No shortcuts. No chukking.

Think about it this way. Sally wants to learn a giant swing on bars. She knows she can't do the skill today but there is no doubt in her mind that she will be doing it in six months or less.

So does Sally see herself as someone who can't do giants? No, of course not. Sally sees herself as someone who will be doing giants within six months. Instead of focusing on what she is not, Sally focuses on what she is -- a talented gymnast learning giants.

So she gets to work, knowing that her job is to accumulate as much useful experience as possible in as short a time as possible. Sometimes she messes up. She figures out what she did wrong and moves on. Thus, messing up is a useful experience because now Sally has learned what does not work.

Within six months, guess what? Sally is zipping over the bar with ease. Just like she knew she would.

I got to where I am because of self-confidence.
I'll get to where I want to be with the same self-confidence.

THE GOING FOR IT! SELF-CONFIDENCE LOOP

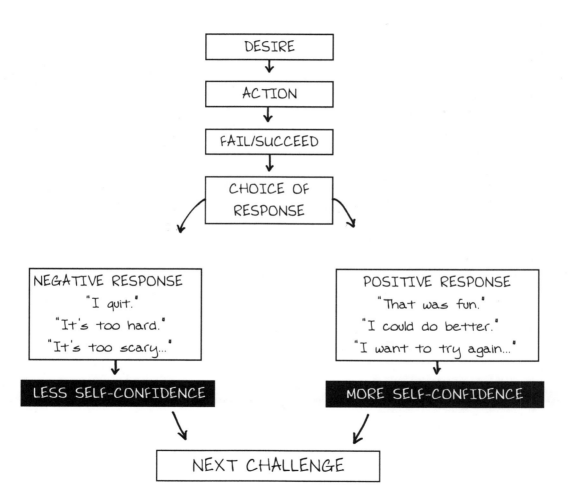

THE GOING FOR IT! CONFIDENCE LOOP

"One of the best things that ever happened to me was to miss making the regional team because of a blown pommel horse routine. I made sure that never happened again."
Chris Jenkins - Level 1

Everyone has a set amount of talent. We will never get more. Some people have learned how to develop their talent more than others. This is why less-talented people frequently out-perform their more talented friends.

We all start out with a desire to pursue these talents. So we go out and challenge ourselves. A first flip on mom and dad's bed perhaps. (Yes, I know you never do that.)

If we fail we have two choices. We can get excited to try again or we can think, "That was too hard," and quit doing flips. If we succeed we also have two choices. We can get excited to try again or we can think, "That was too scary," and quit doing flips.

We are now on the positive or negative side of the confidence loop. We either come through this experience with more desire or less. If we come through on the positive side we get to take on our next challenge with a little more confidence, self-esteem and determination. If we come through on the negative side we have to face our next challenge with a little less confidence, self-esteem, and determination. This pattern repeats itself every time we are faced with a challenge.

After a few thousand times through the confidence loop we are either filled with self-confidence or self-doubt, depending upon which side of the loop we chose to travel most of the time. Remember the important word is _CHOSE_.

I chose my responses to ups and downs very carefully.

Do
The Best You Can
Right Now

As You Get Better
You Can
Do Better

CONFIDENCE TAKER #1 - "I'M NOT GOOD ENOUGH"

*"I know where I want to be in 10 years but
I concentrate on what I need to do in the next 30 minutes."*
Paul Fulton - Level 3

Some gymnasts make the mistake of only thinking about the dream gymnast they are going to be "some day." As a result they convince themselves that who they are right now is in some way inferior. Therefore, they can never be happy until they reach their goal, achieve their dream, and make all their ambitions a reality. It is pretty much impossible to be a confident person when you see yourself as "not good enough".

Winners don't think this way. Sure, they have a clear idea in their mind of where they are heading. Winners know they don't get to be a great college gymnast without being a great 8-year-old, 12-year-old and 16-year-old gymnast first. So right now they are excited to be doing great kips, beautiful back handsprings, and elegant front walkovers. One day they are going to be an awesome 18-year-old gymnast. But that's then -- this is now. So today they are going to be the best 10-, 12-, 14-, or 16-year-old gymnast they can be.

Ask yourself this simple question 50 times a workout:

What is the best I can be right now?

What is the best warm-up I can do? How can I be a better listener when my coach is correcting my performance? How can I be the best teammate? How can I push myself a little harder during this conditioning? How can I point my toes, straighten my leg, or extend my handstand a little more -- **right now?**

My job is to be the best I can be right now.

Look
to others
and say,
"I can learn how to do that"

Don't look
to others
and say,
"I'll never be that good"

CONFIDENCE TAKER # 2 - COMPARING YOURSELF TO OTHERS

"I'm not an idiot. I know I won't make it to the Olympics at my age.
But I can see myself medaling in vault at an NCAA championships."
Rebecca Clifford.

"If I were as good as Shannon I would have more confidence," says Margo. Meanwhile, Shannon is thinking, "I would be so confident if I were as good as Becky." Becky, at the other end of the gym, is thinking, "I wish I was a beginner again like Margo, I had so much confidence back when I was a beginner."

It has been said that the root of all unhappiness is comparing ourselves to others.

Comparing yourself to someone else and feeling like a big old loser dufus because you are not as "lucky," is not a good thing. Wanting to be as good as someone else and using them as a role model to move towards is a good thing.

When we compare ourselves to others we are saying, "I am not good enough." And we lose confidence.

When we look to others as role models we are saying "I am good enough to get there." And we gain confidence.

I'm good, and I'm getting better.

Confidence
Does Not Eliminate
Your Fears
But
It does Give You
The Power
To Handle Them

CONFIDENCE TAKER # 3 - FEAR

"I used to think fear was a bad thing until Mark spoke at our gym.
Now I see it as just another one of the challenges of gymnastics."
Timothy Dobsen - Level 4

Imagine if you had a crystal ball in your gym. Every time you got a little scared to do something you could go over to the crystal ball, peer inside and look three minutes into the future. If you saw yourself successfully performing the skill you were afraid of you would no longer be scared. If you saw yourself crashing, you would keep working drills until the picture in the crystal ball changed.

Wouldn't it be great to have a crystal ball like this? Well, you do!

It's your self-confidence. You don't need to look into a crystal ball to predict the future. You just need to pay attention to your own gut feelings.

"If it don't feel right, chances are it ain't right!"

Pardon my grammar.

If your head is filled with pictures of failing, messing up, and getting injured then you are simply not ready to face the challenge before you. You must first change those pictures in your head. Maybe you're not physically ready and need to do more drills or be spotted a few more times. Or maybe you are physically ready but haven't taken a mental time-out to get your mind together. Either way, don't ignore your instincts. Change the picture first and then take on the challenge.

I never ignore my inner intelligence.

Self-Confidence
And
Self-Doubt
Are Not The Result
Of What Happens To Us
But Of What
We Choose To Do
About
What Happens To Us

CONFIDENCE TAKER # 4 - FAILURE

*"I think the greatest challenge in gymnastics is not
making something that is really minor into a big problem."*
Amanda Tompkins - Level 8

Confidence is not the result of always succeeding and never making mistakes. If it were, then there would not be a single confident person on the planet. Everybody makes mistakes, everybody messes up, everybody gets injured occasionally, and everybody gets scared sometimes.

So why are some people spilling over with confidence, while others drown in self-doubt?

Confident people accept the fact they are not perfect. So they expect to mess up occasionally, and they expect to succeed occasionally. They know that who they will become in 10 years or so will not be a result of how many times they succeeded or messed up or how many times they won or lost. Who they will become will be a result of what they learned from all those experiences.

If they win, they can call it luck and point out that the only reason they won was because everyone else messed up. Or they can simply be grateful. This way, winning teaches them to appreciate their own talent and all the people who helped them develop that talent. This gives them the confidence to want to win again.

If they lose, they can make excuses or blame other people. If they do this, losing teaches them never to take responsibility for their mistakes and failures. Or they can learn to ask themselves what they could have done differently. Now losing teaches them how to fine-tune their training habits. Again, they come through more confident.

Failure teaches me what doesn't work.

What
You Believe
To Be Real
Is
Your Reality

CONFIDENCE TAKER # 5 - SELF-DOUBT

*"Looking back, my biggest regret is
I didn't realize how good I was."*
Mary Johnson.

If we walk around all day thinking about all the terrible things that can go wrong in our lives, we will tend to act in ways to make many of those things a reality.

For instance: Mary is convinced she is a lousy vaulter. By seeing herself as a lousy vaulter she knows there is no point in wasting all that effort in a workout. So Mary will spend two to three hours a week of vault workout time confirming her belief. She actually will train herself to be the lousy vaulter she sincerely believes she is. What she believes to be real she will make real. She says, "I am a lousy vaulter and I always will be," and she's right.

Confident Carrie doesn't operate this way. She bombards herself with images of what she wants to become. She doesn't dwell so much on the fact she's not a great vaulter. She knows she's not a great vaulter, but that's not how she sees herself. She sees herself as someone who is working very hard to become a great vaulter. So at every workout she does all the things necessary to make that her reality. She says, "Today I will train like a great vaulter because one day I will be a great vaulter." And she's right!

Both Mary and Carrie are right. They are both training to make their beliefs a reality. And they both will be successful.

Self-doubt reminds me that I haven't completed all the necessary work to feel confident.

WHAT THIS CHAPTER MEANS TO ME

1. When faced with fear do I:

  A...See it as an opportunity to grow more courageous........................ ☐

  B...See it as a reason to give up.. ☐

2. Failure makes me want to:

  A...Learn what I did wrong and try again.. ☐

  B...Quit in frustration.. ☐

3. When I feel a little self-doubt I:

  A...Visualize what I want and remind myself of my strengths............. ☐

  B...Convince myself I am not good enough...................................... ☐

4. When I watch other gymnasts who are better than me I:

  A...Figure out what I can learn from their performance.................... ☐

  B...Figure I'll never be that good and become discouraged........... ☐

5. When I think about my dreams and how good I'll be one day:

  A...I am inspired to keep setting and achieving my small daily goals. ☐

  B...I get discouraged. I am so far from being the gymnast I want to be. ☐

What does this tell me about how I develop my confidence?

THE LAST WORD

So confidence it seems is not the result of never making mistakes. Everybody makes mistakes. Confidence is choosing to learn from mistakes and remain focused on the original goal. When we choose to see mistakes and failures as temporary learning experiences we can learn the lesson without any damage to our self-confidence.

In other words, winners do not see themselves as a collection of all their mistakes and failures. Winners see themselves as a collection of all the important lessons they have learned from past mistakes, failures and successes.

Therefore, when winners go to meets and lose, it never occurs to them that everyone is looking at them as a big old failure. That is simply not the way they look at themselves.

They are learning how to be a great gymnast. Losing meets occasionally is one of the less enjoyable, yet necessary lessons they must learn from. Therefore, they don't feel the need to seek pity with temper tantrums, moodiness, or excessive crying. Sure, they lost the meet, but not their self-respect. And what if they win? No need to draw attention to themselves by boasting about their win. If people noticed that they won, that's nice! If they didn't, it's not the end of their world.

CHAPTER 5

ATTITUDE

The Double Win Attitude

The Single Win Attitude

The Process Oriented Athlete

A Winner's Attitude For Life

Choose Your Attitude - Fearless Or Courageous?

Rage Or Anger?

Crying Or Trying?

Envy Or Admiration?

Sciving Or Striving?

Dump Your "Have To" Attitude

Toss Your "I Can't" Attitude

Trash Your "I'm Trying" Attitude

Sling Your "It's Too Hard" Attitude

Going
For The Gold
Is More
Important
Than
Getting The Gold

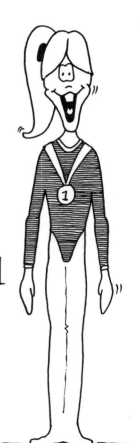

THE DOUBLE WIN ATTITUDE

*"Sometimes I look at pictures of Chaney Umphrey and think,
man if all I get out of gymnastics is a body like that, that wouldn't be so bad."*
Robert Webber - Level 2

Winners have figured out an important lesson. They know there are no absolute guarantees they definitely will get what they want.

So why do so many gymnasts work so hard anyway?

Why not?

Think about it. What is the worst that could possibly happen to our winner? Let's say, after a lifetime of developing a beautiful body, sharpening an incredible talent, learning from amazing people and becoming an inspiration for countless others, our winner fails to reach his dreams.

Then what is he left with?

A beautiful body, an incredible talent, a network of amazing friends, and countless numbers of grateful inspired winners around him. Not bad!

When we give 100% to reaching our dreams we never really fail in the long run.

I may not always win but I refuse to be a loser.

Winners Celebrate Winning
Losers Celebrate Defeating

THE SINGLE WIN ATTITUDE

"I used to think that the only thing in life was winning. I wasn't much fun to be around.
Winning is still important but you have to have some balance in your life."
Beth Spacey - Coach

Did you ever run into one of those folks who r-e-a-l-l-y love to win? And when they do, they make sure you are r-e-a-l-l-y aware you lost? Unpleasant people aren't they?

For them, competition is not about the challenge of being the best they can be. Instead, it is all about being better than you. If, by chance, you should win, they won't congratulate you. They will however, make some snide remark about how the judges were easy on you, or how your leotard is ugly. This is their little way of putting you down and somehow getting back on top. How sad!

Somewhere along the line these folks learned that unless they are number-one they are somehow inferior. They can't like themselves until they are number-one. So they spend 99% of their lives walking around disliking themselves. No wonder they are miserable.

On the occasions that they do win, they are boastful, rude and arrogant. They end up with the trophies, the medals and the ribbons, but no friends.

Not much of a win, is it?

Winning means everything to me, but it's not the only thing.

Do You
Put Off Enjoying Music
Until The End Of The Song,
Or
Do You
Enjoy The Whole Thing?

Pursuing Your Dreams
Should Work The Same Way

THE PROCESS ORIENTED ATHLETE
"You have to enjoy the process of learning."
Patty Stotzheim - Coach

Sally says, "I'll be a happy person when I win. In the meantime, I'm gonna be a grumpy, moody, miserable person. That way, everyone will know I'm serious about my goals and they will stop bugging me about why I never seem to win."

Steven says, "I'm a gymnast because I love being a gymnast. I didn't start gymnastics to win medals and ribbons. I started because I love being upside down, I love jumping over stuff, and I love climbing to the top of anything I can climb to the top of. However, since I started competing I find I like winning medals and ribbons too. So now every day I focus on what I love to do. Flipping upside down, jumping and climbing. Except now I do it in the form of gymnastics routines. And I do those routines the best I know how. As a result, I win quite a few medals and ribbons."

Steven has figured out an important lesson.

It's a miserable struggle trying to succeed at something you don't love 100%.

He knows that in order to do your best at anything you have to love the whole process, not just the end result.

I love gymnastics. Winning is a great bonus.

Who
We Become
Is The Greatest Reward
For
Achieving Our Dreams
Not
What We Get

A WINNER'S ATTITUDE FOR LIFE
"You have to work hard and practice; you have to want to do it."
Sarah Tomlinson - Level 5

So is it really possible that the main reason for setting goals and having big dreams is not so much the achievement of the dream itself, but rather what we can become by pushing ourselves to achieve a meaningful dream?

In a word; yes!

Every day you are training to become two things:

1. A gymnast
2. A winner

You will be a gymnast until you are about 25 (maybe).

You will be a winner your whole life (hopefully).

It's a great feeling to wake up in the morning knowing that you get to spend the rest of your life with a hard working, goal-oriented, compassionate winner.

Especially when that winner is you.

It's overcoming the struggle to win that makes me a champion, not the win itself.

*If
You've Never
Been Scared
Then Chances Are
You've
Never Pushed Yourself*

CHOOSE YOUR ATTITUDE - FEARLESS OR COURAGEOUS?
"When people call me fearless I just kind of smile. If only they knew."
Roger Porter - Level 1

There really are only two kinds of fearless people in the world. One, I am very familiar with, because he lives in my house. If I didn't stop him he would happily run into traffic, shove things up his nose that do not belong up noses, and would gladly dive head first into the toilet bowl. Pretty stupid, eh? Of course, I do stop him. He's my two-year-old son Timothy.

The other kind of fearless person? Well, somebody whose idea of adventure is a night at home with a giant bucket of Ben and Jerry's Chunky Monkey ice cream, and a super size Slurpee never gets scared. And why do they never get scared? Because they never push themselves.

In other words, the only truly fearless people in the world are either stupid (like a two year old - you're allowed to be stupid when you're two) or lazy (like a couch potato 12-year-old who doesn't care if they are ever good at anything.)

Courageous people are not fearless. Quite the opposite, in fact. They have many fears. After all, if you are always pushing yourself to stretch your limits, you are bound to encounter fears all the time. Courageous people are called courageous not because they ignore or avoid their fears but because they face up to them and deal with them.

I am not fearless. I am couragous.

Winners
Turn Anger Into
Determination

Losers
Turn Anger Into
Dismay

RAGE OR ANGER?

"I get a little mad when I mess up at meets."
Kristi Dobra - Level 10

In the middle of his sixth attempt to complete a skill on pommel horse, Freddie's hand slips. He flies off the side of the horse, flips upside own once, and lands in an unattractive heap on the mat. Oh no! Freddy's gonna blow.

As his teammates back up out of harm's way, Freddy starts his usual routine of kicking the horse and yelling at the guy who invented it. Freddy does this a lot. Is it helpful? Apparently not. He's been throwing temper tantrums for five years and pommel horse is still his worst event. So why does he do it? Ask him (when he calms down) and he will tell you that this is just the way he is. Well, "the way he is" is affecting the workout of everyone in the gym, including his own.

Is it OK to get angry? Sure it is. Anger is a normal reaction to frustrating circumstances. We can use the energy that comes with anger to focus our attention on a problem that needs to be addressed. Freddy is not expressing anger. He is raging furiously out of control. When he focuses away from the problem and just on the frustration he is feeling, he is not doing a thing to solve the problem that got him frustrated in the first place. So Freddy's problem gets a little worse, and Freddy's tantrums get a little louder. The cycle goes on.

I don't let anger distract me from my goals.

You
Can't
Be Crying
And Trying
At The Same Time

CRYING OR TRYING?

"I know some people get upset at meets.
That only seems to make things worse."
Kelly Straka - Level 9

For the fifth time in a row, Mandy lands a little short on her full twist. She's upset. She doesn't want to do it... she hates it when she does it... it bugs her coach when she does it, but she just can't seem to stop herself. She starts to cry.

30 seconds later she is well into a full-blown, seven hanky sniffler. Her workout has come to a temporary halt while Mandy has a mini-nervous breakdown.

So is crying a bad thing? Well, yes and no. As an emotional release, crying certainly seems help some gymnasts let go of their frustrations. It provides them with a transition period; a chance to work through the frustration and get on with the task of dealing with the problem that bought on the sniffles in the first place. However, during the 3 to 33 minutes it can take to recover from a good sniffle session, nothing gets done.

It would certainly be better for Mandy if she could switch quickly from frustration to determination without the need for a long sniffle bridge between the two.

The clock on the wall doesn't wait for me to get control of myself.

If You Are Waiting
Until You Succeed
Before You Stop Being Jealous Of Others
You Will Never
Succeed

When You
No Longer Feel
The Need To Be Jealous
You Will Have Succeeded

ENVY OR ADMIRATION?

" Iused to want to be someone else when I was younger.
Now I just want to be me; but a better version."
Debbie Francis - Level 8

Jenny is so envious of Judy. "I wish I could tumble the way Judy does," she says.

Judy is so envious of Jenny. "I wish I could swing bars the way Jenny does," she says.

While both Jenny and Judy are busy being jealous of each other, Julie is at the other end of the gym. She loves watching both Jenny and Judy compete and work out.

Once she spent a whole bar session studying the way Jenny shapes her body on a tap swing. She trained herself to do the same shapes and, as a result, improved her own bar swing. Another time, she noticed that Judy arches more in her shoulders than in her lower back on a front handspring. She tried the same thing herself and was able to front tumble much faster.

Julie has a great deal of admiration for her two friends, but she is not envious of either of them. By admiring them she can learn from them.

I wouldn't want to be anyone else but me.

Laziness
Is The Habit Of
Resting
Before
You Get Tired

CARE TO
JOIN US?

SCIVING OR STRIVING?
"You have to practice, work hard , and have dedication."
Ashley Gable - Level 7

Sciving is British slang for being lazy.

A sciver works hard only when it is convenient to work hard. Say for instance, when their hands are not sore, their shoulders don't ache, or their mood is just right.

Hey! Big deal. Who can't work hard when the conditions are perfect?

One of the real tests of winners is how hard they work when it is not easy.

In the last half hour of workout, when everyone else is complaining about being tired, winners push themselves to make the most of the last 30 minutes. In the middle of the summer, when it is 110 degrees in the gym, it is the winner who drinks plenty of water, towels off, and gets back up one more time. At the meet, when the whole team blows beam/pommel horse, it is the winner who picks up the team's spirits and gets everyone focused on the next event.

Don't get me wrong. Winner's don't ignore obvious signs to rest. They know when to rest. This means they know the difference between pain and discomfort. They know the difference between tragedy and inconvenience. And they know the difference between problems and challenges. Scivers, unfortunately, can't tell the difference.

I know when to rest and I know when to push.

Winner Vocabulary 101

"I have to."

Really means:

"My coaches and parents make me do this stuff. I have no choice in the matter. Therefore I also have no responsibility. So if things don't work out it's not my fault, 'cause I'm not in charge."

Change to:

"I choose to because I want to."

DUMP YOUR "HAVE TO" ATTITUDE

"When I realized I didn't have to do conditioning it became a lot easier."
Linda Armstrong - Level 9

Here's some great news!

You don't have to do conditioning. You don't have to do flexibility work. You don't have to work out when you are tired. You don't have to miss all those cool school functions. In fact, you don't even have to come to workout at all.

However, winners do all these things. Not because they have to, but because they want to. That doesn't mean they necessarily like doing these things. They just do them because it's part of the price they pay for achieving their dreams. No whining. No fussing. No complaining. They just do them.

Think of all the time-consuming things you do every day that you just take for granted as part of the price for living on planet Earth. You don't have to shower, but you chose to because you don't want to smell bad. You don't have to breath in and out all day, every day, but you chose to because the alternative would involve passing out several times a day. The same goes for eating. What a time-waster that is, but you wouldn't want to stop eating, would you?

These things become a burden to us only when we feel some cruel outside force is making us do things we don't want to do. When we take responsibility for all these actions and admit that we don't have to do any of them, but we do choose to do them, suddenly they are not so bad.

I don't work hard because I have to. I work hard because I want to .

Winner Vocabulary 101

"I can't."

Really means:

"I don't know whether I can or not, but I do know I can't be bothered to learn."

Change to:

"How can I learn?"

TOSS YOUR "I CAN'T" ATTITUDE
"If you say can't it's like you're giving up."
Christie Black - Level 5

Isn't it an exciting world we live in?

Think of all the wonderful things there are to learn and do. When we are born we are just this tiny helpless lump and can do hardly anything for ourselves. But as we grow we learn to walk, and then talk, and before you know it we are doing forward rolls and cartwheels. Not long after that comes our first back handspring, followed within a year or so by a back tuck. And then twists, and then....

Tiny babies do not concern themselves with full twists on floor. They tend to live in the moment. They tackle today's challenge. They don't think "I can't roll over." They just keep trying until they roll over. A 10-month-old baby doesn't worry about never walking. They just keep practicing until they can.

We could learn quite a bit from these little guys.

The very fact that we can't do something is all the reason in the world we need to get on with trying to learn how. And once we have learned how, hey, let's find something else we can't do, and learn how to do that as well.

I get excited about all the things I can't do today, but will be able to do soon.

Winner Vocabulary 101

"I'm trying."

Really means:

"I feel like I'm working hard. That should be enough to satisfy you, so get off my case."

Change to:

"This isn't working. I'll try something different."

TRASH YOUR "I'M TRYING" ATTITUDE
"Trying sounds like whining. I don't like whining."
Eric Boon - Level 3

"But I'm trying to keep my legs straight," says Amanda after the 37th time today her coach mentions her bent legs.

Well, guess what Amanda? What you are trying "ain't" working. So stop trying and do something different.

When we keep insisting to our coaches that we are trying, what we are really saying is: this is all the effort I am willing to put into fixing this problem. If it doesn't fix the problem, tough luck. I'm not willing to do something different.

In almost all cases, the word "trying" can be replaced with the word "failing" and the sentence would actually be more accurate.

Now Amanda says, "But I'm failing to keep my legs straight."

Ah! Now we can go somewhere. Amanda now is admitting to herself that she is not achieving the desired result of keeping her legs straight. Apparently, just getting up and trying to keep them straight (37 times in a row) doesn't work. So now she can give up on what does not work and concentrate on something that might.

In other words: Stop trying, start doing.

I don't try my best... I do my best.

Winner Vocabulary 101

"It's too hard."

Really means:

"No way am I willing to work this hard. But I don't want to lower my goals either. So I guess I'll just whine to everyone about how hard this is, while not achieving any of my goals."

Change to:

"Achieving my goals is going to take more effort than I expected. I will increase my effort."

SLING YOUR "IT'S TOO HARD" ATTITUDE
"Keep your cool; stay positive."
Gina Candora - Level 5

Do you have a few "It's too hard" whiners in your gym?

They just haven't figured it out have they? Going after dreams requires dedication, perseverance and sacrifice. And that is hard work, no doubt about it!

However, giving up on a dream and living a life that never taps into our talents means always feeling sort of empty inside. And guess what? That's hard, too!

The choice we have to make is not between an easy life or a hard one. The choice is: which hardship do I prefer?

Spending a day in Disney World is hard. You'll walk miles in that place. But we don't mind because a day in Disney World is fun. Life only becomes "too" hard when we stop having fun.

If all the hard work you are doing is not moving you in the direction of you dreams, you will find yourself whining about things being too hard. However, if every day you know you are making your dreams come true you'll be working very hard, but you won't call it hard work. You'll call it fun.

When we really want something bad enough, nothing is too hard.

I never expected any of this to be easy.

WHAT THIS CHAPTER MEANS TO ME

1. I view fear as an indicator that I am:

    A... *pushing the edges of my abilities and extending my talent*................. ❏

    B... *trying too hard and that I should back off a little*.................................. ❏

2. If I am trying but not succeeding, that tells me:

    A... *I am trying the wrong thing so I change what I am doing*.................... ❏

    B... *that I am not "lucky enough" to be able to learn things easily*.............. ❏

3. When I think of all the things I can't do I:

    A... *get excited to learn new things*... ❏

    B... *want to quit in dismay*.. ❏

4. There are some things about gymnastics I don't particularly like doing. So I:

    A... *accept them as part of the price I pay to be in this great sport*............ ❏

    B... *whine about them every time my coach "makes me" do them*............ ❏

5. When I get upset about something in training or in competition I:

    A... *use the emotion to make me even more determined*......................... ❏

    B... *wish things were not so hard all the time*..................................... ❏

What does this tell me about my general attitude?

THE LAST WORD

Imagine you want a new bike. You spend the entire summer (eight hours a day) stocking shelves at the local supermarket. In September, you get your new bike. That weekend you and a friend ride over to Dairy Queen. While inside, both your bikes get stolen. Your friend (the rich kid who gets a new bike every year) says "bummer, guess we will have to walk home." You, on the other hand, are going out of your mind with panic.

Why the difference in reactions? Simply put, your friend had very little of herself invested in her bike, so it was easy for her to give it up. You, however, invested an entire summer of your life in your bike. No way are you letting it go that easy.

While your friend sits on the steps of the D.Q. slurping down her frosty, you are running around talking to everyone who might have seen your bike being stolen. Within 15 minutes you've found both bikes.

When we invest very little of ourselves in our dreams it is easy to quit. When we invest a great deal of ourselves we are bound to get emotional about the ups and downs, but it's unlikely that we will quit. The crashes anger us, the tough skills frustrate us, and the defeats disappoint us, but we keep at it because this is our dream. When we hit that routine or win that meet, the pride we feel is in direct proportion to the investment we made.

CHAPTER 6

TEAM

Dependent/Independent/Interdependent

Together **E**veryone **A**chieves **M**ore

Team Sports

Playing Your Position

Be The Most Important Member Of Your Team

Heroes

Always Have A Better Attitude Than Your Team's Average

There
Is No
Such Thing
As An
Individual Sport

DEPENDENT/INDEPENDENT/INTERDEPENDENT

"In gymnastics you set goals for yourself,
but you also encourage and help your teammates."
Becky Clement - Level 4

Billy depends 100% on everyone else to constantly push him all the time. He is quite a drain on the team. He needs constant support from coaches and teammates, but is unable or unwilling to offer support back in return. A dependent gymnast like Billy has a "What can you do for me?" attitude towards his team.

Millie, on the other hand, is more independent. She gets to the gym on time, focuses on her goals, and works hard to achieve those goals. She is very self-motivated and rarely needs to be pushed. Because she is so independent she believes everybody else should feel the same way. So Millie doesn't offer her teammates a great deal of support. Millie has an "If I can do it by myself, so can you," attitude toward her team.

Jilly also sees herself as independent. But more importantly, she also considers herself to be interdependent. She has confidence in herself but knows she can do much better when she accepts the support of a good team. In return, Jilly gives back to her team the same kind of support and strength she receives. She has an "I could do OK by myself, but I can do much better as part of a great team," attitude.

The strength I give to my team is the strength my team returns.

A
Team Is Only
As Strong
As Its
Average Member

Together Everyone Achieves More

"When the entire team is strong everybody competes better."
Karen Erickson - Level 5

Imagine if everyone on Billy's team were just like him. 30 dependent, unmotivated, directionless lumps sitting around the gym waiting for their coach to tell them what to do. Does this sound like the make up of a highly successful team?

Would it be better if the whole team was like Millie? 30 independent gymnasts all working hard toward their own self-indulgent personal goals. All competing against each other. Never sharing ideas. Never supporting each other. Never asking for help. If one of them wins a meet the rest get jealous and start thinking of ways to bring that winner down.

How about a team of 30 Jillys? All with personal goals that are in some way linked to the central goal of the team. As they work hard to achieve their own goals they share ideas and offer support to their teammates. In doing so they get great ideas and support right back. When one of them wins they all get together and figure out what they can learn from that win. This makes every member of the team a little better and the team a little stronger.

Which team would you rather be a member of?

I am moving in the same direction as my team.

A Rose
Does Not Grow Well
In A
Bed Of Weeds

TEAM SPORTS
"I can't imagine doing this in a gym all by myself."
Melissa Lopez - Level 10

It would be easy to fool yourself into thinking gymnastics is not a team sport. After all, we don't run around a big grassy field or wooden court passing a ball to each other trying to kick, dunk, shoot, or bounce it into a net, do we?

We do, however, rely upon each other for support and inspiration. Our success as a team does depend our individual performances. But those individual performances owe a great deal to the team that inspired them.

Remember:

Behind every individual success is a team effort.
And behind every team success are the efforts of every individual.

Gold medal winners owe a piece of their win to the team that encouraged and supported them. Likewise, a winning team wins because of the combined effort of every member of the team -- not just the top scorers.

I can tap into the energy of my team.

*You Can
Help Raise The
Team Score
In More Ways Than Just
Competing Well*

PLAYING YOUR POSITION
"Meets are what it's all about."
Kurt Flannders - Level 4

In gymnastics we don't play the usual positions you hear about in other sports, such as quarterback, shortstop, or point guard. Our playing positions are more subtle.

For example:

"ON DECK"

This is the gymnast up next to compete. Her job is to be off by herself running routines through her head and generally getting herself mentally ready to compete.

"COMPETITOR"

This, of course, is the gymnast on the apparatus going through a routine.

"COOL DOWN"

This gymnast has just finished her routine. She is taking a couple of minutes to go over the routine in her head. She is making mental notes of corrections. She also is getting herself out of a competitor's state of mind and into that of her next role.

"SUPPORT"

This is the remainder of the team. Comprised of those who have already competed the event and those who are not up for awhile. Their job is to support the competitor. They do this by moving and adjusting apparatus and cheering on their competing teammate.

I play my position well.

The Most Important Member Of Your Team Is You

BE THE MOST IMPORTANT MEMBER OF YOUR TEAM

"I cheer for my teammates because I know how it feels when they cheer for me."
Kathy Guy - Level 8

"Be the most important member of my team?

"Yeah, right!" I hear you say.

You are probably thinking that's impossible. After all, you rarely are the highest scorer. So what?

I once worked with a team whose most important influence wasn't even on the team. She was a class kid. She was 13 years old and she was blind. Yes, that's right - blind. She was enrolled in a regular class with all the other 13 year olds and came in once a week on a Wednesday evening. Her mom would come out onto the gym floor to help the coach, but otherwise this 13-year-old blind girl did everything the rest of the class did.

So what day of the week do you think the team kids worked hardest, whined the least and complained less? I hope you guessed Wednesday.

That's right. This blind girl's courage and determination was such an inspiration to the rest of the kids in the gym that, without a doubt, she was the most important gymnast in the gym that night.

We all can't be the highest scoring gymnast on our team but we certainly can push up the team score by inspiring everyone around us.

The most important thing I can do for my team is be an inspiration to them.

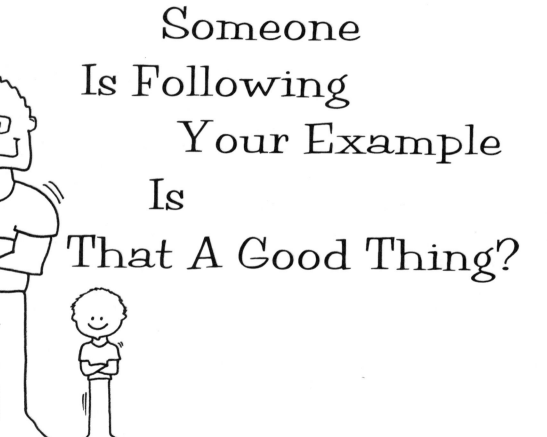

Someone
Is Following
    Your Example
Is
That A Good Thing?

HEROES

"It never occured to me that I am now the kind of person I used to look up to 10 years ago."
Laurie Keaty - Level 10

Have you been competing in gymnastics for a while (say, three years or more)? If so, then whether you know it or not, you are a hero to someone.

Every day in the gym a younger gymnast is looking up to you. She may never tell you, but she watches the way you train. She watches when you get back up on the apparatus after the fifteenth fall on the same skill. She watches you as you prepare yourself to do a scary skill for the first time without a spot. She watches you when you blow a routine at a meet that you knew for sure you were going to hit.

She watches, and she learns.

She learns how her hero bounces back from failure. She learns how her hero pushes herself through a tough workout. She learns how her hero turns defeat into determination.

Then she goes right out and puts into practice all the things her hero has taught her.

I never forget that I am always inspiing others by my actions.

Be
The Strongest Link
In Your
Team

ALWAYS HAVE A BETTER ATTITUDE THAN YOUR TEAM'S AVERAGE

*"The last thing I want to do is slack off at a meet knowing that
someone else has to try harder because I want to be lazy."*
Brad Wall - Level 2

Try this little exercise. No need to share your findings with anyone.

Take a sheet of paper and write down as many positive characteristics about your team as you can think of. Things that are a matter of attitude. Things such as: dedicated, hard workers, energetic, team spirited, determined, that sort of stuff.

Now take one category. We'll use "dedicated" as an example. Give a score of minus ten points to the least dedicated person on your team. Now give ten points to the most dedicated person on your team. With those two extremes in your head, ask yourself what your score would be. Do this with every category. Did you come up with a personal score lower than zero in any category? If so, that is one place where you are holding back your team. What could you do to push yourself into the positive numbers? Are you scoring higher than zero anywhere? Good job. Your are adding to your team's strength.

Imagine if everyone on the team did this. What would start to happen to those averages? They'd start going up, and up, and up....

We have limited control over the scores we get in competition. But we have 100% control over the scores we deserve for attitude. And these scores are every bit as important to the team as the apparatus scores we get at meets.

My team is a little stronger because of me.

WHAT THIS CHAPTER MEANS TO ME

1. The main reason I am a member of my team is because :

    A... *inspiring others by my own actions gives me more determination*........ ☐

    B... *I have to be on a team if I want to compete*................................ ☐

2. My team gives me:

    A... *the reassurance that I have the ability to realize my dreams*............. ☐

    B... *a fun bunch of friends to hang out with and not much else*.................. ☐

3. At meets, my responsibility toward the team is to:

    A... *do everything I can to bring up the team score*........................... ☐

    B... *do the best routines I can*.. ☐

4. I am aware of where my performance/attitude is holding my team back. So I:

    A... *am working hard to improve myself in those areas*........................ ☐

    B... *figure my strengths in other areas balance things out*................... ☐

5. The best way for me to help my teammates is to:

    A... *inspire them with my actions*... ☐

    B... *motivate them with my words*... ☐

What does this tell me about how I view my role on my team?

THE LAST WORD

Let's talk furniture!

A good table needs four strong legs. It can have more if it is a big table, but any less than four would give you a pretty unstable table. (Try saying that five times fast.) These legs must also be of equal strength. Three strong legs and one weak leg means your table is going to collapse sideways sooner or later. Trying to make up for weak legs by adding more weak legs doesn't seem to work well either. Nope! You want a good table, you are going to have to give it good strong legs.

Same thing goes for a gymnastics team. Ever go to a meet where they call the third place team onto the award stand and 24 kids run up? Then they call up the first place team and four kids hop up onto the award stand. How can four kids beat twenty four? The answer is simple. Strong gymnasts make a strong team. You can't make up for weakness by adding more weakness.

Everybody has some kind of strength they can bring to the team. Maybe one member is not the greatest all-arounder, but they can nail vault. Some can't swing bars so well, but man, can they tumble. Even the gymnast that never scores well on any apparatus can be the most valuble member of the team. How? Simply by having the kind of personality that inspires others to their best performance. A good team knows how to bring out the strengths of all it's members.

You can write to Mark at...

Wind Dancer Publications
P.O.Box 263
Perkasie PA 18944

Want to order copies of GFI! "1" or GFI! "2"
or the GFI training journal for your teammates?
Discounts are available for bulk orders.

Call 215 257-4584